BOOKS BY **ROBERT E. DALEY**

A Case for "Threes"
A Simple Plan . . . of Immense Complexity
Armour, Weapons, And Warfare
from Everlasting to Everlasting
Killer Sex
Life or Death, Heaven or Hell, You Choose!
Raptures and Resurrections
Short Tales
So . . . What Happens to the Package?
Study and Interpretation of The Scriptures Made Simple
Surviving Destruction as A Human Being
The Gospel of John
The Gospel of John (Red Edition)
The League of The Immortals
The New Testament - Pauline Revelation
The New Testament - Pauline Revelation Companion
"The World That Then Was . . ." & The Genesis That Now Is
What Color Are You?
What Makes A Christian Flaky?
What Really Happened to Judas Iscariot?
Who YOU Are in Christ . . . RIGHT NOW!

The Enhancement Series

#1 Book of Ecclesiastes
#2 Book of Daniel
#3 Book of Romans
#4 Book of Galatians
#5 Book of Hebrews

The Deeper Things of God Series

#1 The Personage of God
#2 The Personage of Man
#3 The Personage of Christ

The Enhancement Series • Book Two

THE OLD TESTAMENT

BOOK OF DANIEL

ENHANCED

Enjoy the Book of Daniel
as set forth in understandable
language through original
King James Translation
with *Enhancement*

Robert E. Daley

The Larry Czerwonka Company, LLC
Hilo, Hawai‘i

First Edition — November 2014

This book is set in 14-point Garamond

Published by: The Larry Czerwonka Company, LLC
http://czerwonkapublishing.com

Printed in the United States of America

ISBN:0692330089
ISBN-13: 978-0692330081

All scriptures used in this work are taken from the King James Version of the Scriptures.

Introduction

Daniel is considered a Major Prophet among the numerous prophetical authors of the books within the Old Testament. Not because of the size or volume of his work, as is usually the case with Isaiah, Jeremiah, and Ezekiel, but because of the depth and intensity of what God had him to pen.

His book is, by many, considered to be the "Revelation" of the Old Testament. And a number of *subject-trains* from his work make their way into the *roundhouse* of the Book of Revelation, that was written by the Apostle John, when he was exiled onto the Isle of Patmos.

Daniel was a young man when he was taken into captivity, from the Israeli Southern Kingdom of Judah along with his three friends, Hananiah, Azariah, and Mishael. Nebuchadnezzar swept in and removed captives back into Babylon, several times: and Daniel's removal was one of the last.

The more well-known events that the book contains are: the dream about the Statue Image of Kingdoms to come; the Fiery Furnace incident with Shadrach, Meshach, and Abednego; Nebuchadnezzar's Insanity occurrence; the Handwriting on the Wall within the palace; Daniel in the Lion's Den; and History and End-time Events.

The book has been *enhanced* for the purpose of clarity and understanding for the average reader, not for the purpose of altering the word of God.

Please enjoy, and if you do, then share this work with others.

THE BOOK OF
DANIEL

CHAPTER 1

1.   *With*in the third year of the reign of *wicked*
Jehoiakim, *who was the* **king of** *the Jewish, Southern Kingdom of* **Judah,** *who himself was raised up to the throne, in place
of his wicked brother Jehoahas, by Pharaoh-necho, who was the
king of Egypt; and Jehoiakim was carried away by the Pharaoh
into Egypt.* (II Kings 23:34-36 & II Chronicles 36:1-4) *At that time, there*
came **Nebuchadnezzar,***who was the Gentile* **king of** *the*
Babylon*ian Empire* **unto** *the city of* **Jerusalem, and** *he*
besieged it *with his troops.*
2.   **And the Lord** *God Almighty,* **gave Jehoiakim,**
the **king of** *the Jewish, Southern Kingdom of* **Judah into
his hand,** *and thus a seventy year long captivity began for the
Nation of Israel;* (Jeremiah 25:1-11) *along* **with part of the vessels of the house of God, which he** *then* **carried** *off*
**into the land of Shinar, to the house of his god.
And he brought the vessels** *back to Babylon, and put
them* **into the treasure house of his god.**
3.   **And** *after they had returned to Babylon,* **the king,**
Nebuchadnezzar, **spake unto Ashpenaz** *who was* **the
master of his eunuchs, that he should bring** *forth*
certain of the children of Israel, *(in fulfillment of what*

the prophet Isaiah had spoken), *(Isaiah 39:1-8)* and *also* of the king's seed, and of the *various* princes *as well.*

4.   Children in whom *there was* no blemish, but *rather, that were* well-favored, and skilful in all wisdom, and cunning in knowledge, and *the* understanding *of* science, and such as *had an* ability in them to stand in the king's palace, and *such as to* whom they might teach the learning and the tongue of the Chaldeans.

5.   And the king appointed them a daily provision of the king's meat, and of the wine which he *himself* drank. *And in* so *doing, was* nourishing them *for* three years, that at the end *of that time* thereof they might stand before the king.

6.   Now among these *that were chosen* were *there* of the *Israeli* children of *the Southern Kingdom of* Judah, *four men named* Daniel, *and* Hananiah, *and* Mishael, and Azariah.

7.   Unto whom *Ashpenaz,* the prince of the eunuchs gave names. For he gave unto Daniel *the name* of Belteshazzar. And to Hananiah, *the name* of Shadrach. And to Mishael, *the name* of Meshach. And to Azariah, *the name* of Abednego.

8.   But Daniel purposed in his heart that he would not defile himself with the portion of the king's meat, nor with the wine which he drank. Therefore he requested of the prince of the

eunuchs, that he might not defile himself *with these victuals*.

9.   Now God had brought Daniel into favor and tender love with *Ashpenaz, who is* the prince of the eunuchs.

10.   And the prince of the eunuchs said unto Daniel, I fear my lord, *for* the *wrath of the* king, who *himself* hath appointed your meat and your drink. For why should he see your faces *far* worse *to his* liking than the *other* children which *are* of your sort? Then shall ye *put me in jeopardy, and* make *me* endanger my head to the king.

11.   Then said Daniel *un*to Melzar, whom the prince of the eunuchs, *Ashpenaz,* had set over Daniel, *and over* Hananiah, *and* Mishael, and Azariah,

12.   Prove thy servants, I beseech thee, *for only* ten days. And let them give us pulse to eat, *which is vegetables and grains,* and *give us only* water to drink.

13.   *And* then let our countenances be looked upon before thee, and *compare them with* the countenance of the *other* children that eat of the portion of the king's meat *that is given unto them.* And *then* as thou seest *with thine own eyes,* deal with thy servants.

14.   So he consented *un*to them in this matter, and *he* proved them *for* ten days.

15.   And at the end of *the* ten days their countenance appeared *much* fairer and fatter in *the* flesh

than all *of* the *other* children which did eat the portion of the king's meat.

16.   Thus Melzar *permanently* took away the portion of their meat *that came from the king*, and the
wine that they should drink; and gave them pulse
instead.

17.   As for these four *Israeli* children, God gave
them knowledge and skill in all learning and wisdom *beyond the other children*. And Daniel had understanding in *the area of* all visions and dreams.

18.   Now at the end of the days that the king
had said *that* he should bring them in, *which was
three years time*, then *Ashpenaz,* the prince of the eunuchs, brought them in before *king* Nebuchadnezzar.

19.   And the king *took his time, and* communed
with them. And among them all *there* was found
none like Daniel, *and* Hananiah, *and* Mishael, and
Azariah. Therefore stood they before the king.

20.   And in all matters of wisdom *and* understanding, that the king inquired of them, he
found them ten times better than all *of* the magicians *and* astrologers that *were* in all *of* his realm.

21.   And Daniel continued *even* unto the first
year of king Cyrus, *who was king of the Persian Empire.*

CHAPTER 2

1. And in the second year of the reign of Nebuchadnezzar, *which is about one year after Daniel and his friends were taken captive,* Nebuchadnezzar dreamed dreams, wherewith his spirit was *greatly* troubled, and his sleep *did* brake from him.

2. Then the king commanded *his servants* to call *for* the magicians, and the astrologers, and the sorcerers, and the Chaldeans. *And* for *them* to show *unto* the king his dreams, *was his request.* So they came and stood before the king.

3. And the king said unto them, I have dreamed a dream, and my spirit was *greatly* troubled, *and my desire is* to know the dream.

4. Then spake the Chaldeans to the king in Syriac, *or the Aramaic language;* O king, live for ever. Tell thy servants the dream *that thou hast had,* and we will *then* show *unto thee* the interpretation *thereof.*

5. The king answered and said *un*to the Chaldeans, The thing is *now clean* gone from me. If ye will not make known unto me *what* the dream *actually was,* with the interpretation thereof *as well, then* ye shall be cut in*to* pieces, and your houses shall be made a dunghill.

6. But if ye *shall clearly* show *unto me* the dream, and *then* the interpretation thereof, ye shall receive

of me *tremendous* gifts and rewards and great honour. Therefore show *unto* me *now*, the dream, and
the interpretation thereof *as well.*

7.   They answered *once* again and said, Let the
king *first* tell his servants *what* the dream *actually was*,
and we will *then* show *unto thee* the interpretation of
it.

8.   The king answered and said, I know of *a*
certainty that ye would *attempt to stall me, and to* gain
the time, because ye *can* see *that* the thing is *truly*
gone from me.

9.   But if ye will not make known unto me the
dream, *there is but* one decree for you, *and that is
death*. For ye have prepared lying and corrupt
words to speak *as ye stand* before me, *un*til the time
be changed. Therefore tell me the dream *now*, and
I shall know that ye can show me the interpretation thereof *also.*

10.   The Chaldeans answered before the king,
and said, There is not a man *anywhere* upon the *face
of all of the* earth that can show *unto* the king's *satis-
faction concerning this* matter. Therefore *there is* no
king, *nor* lord, nor ruler, *that* has *ever* asked such
things, at *any time, of* any magician, or astrologer,
or Chaldean.

11.   And *it is* a rare thing that the king *should* re-
quireth *the impossible.* And there is *truly* none other

individual that can show it before the king, except *only* the gods, whose dwelling is not with flesh *and blood*.

12.   For this cause the king was *extremely* angry and very furious, and commanded *unto his servants* to *utterly* destroy all *of* the wise *men* of Babylon.

13.   And the decree went forth that *all of* the wise *men that dwelt in Babylon* should be slain. And they sought *after* Daniel and his fellows *Hananiah, and Mishael, and Azariah* to be slain.

14.   Then Daniel answered with *godly* counsel and wisdom to Arioch, *who was* the captain of the king's guard, which was gone forth *by decree*, to slay *all of* the wise *men* of Babylon;

15.   He answered and said *un*to Arioch the king's captain, Why *is* the decree *of death coming* so hast*ily* from the king? Then Arioch made *all of* the *details of the* thing known to Daniel.

16.   Then Daniel went in, and desired of the king that he would give *unto* him *just a little* time, and that he would *then* show *unto* the king the in-terpretation.

17.   Then Daniel went *on home* to his house, and made the thing known to Hananiah, *and to* Mishael, and *to* Azariah, his *fellow* companions.

18.   That *through prayer,* they would desire *and peti-tion* mercies of the God of heaven concerning this

secret *thing. And,* that Daniel and his *beloved* fellows should not perish with the rest of the wise *men* of Babylon.

19.   Then was the *dream's* secret revealed unto Daniel *by the Lord,* in a night vision. Then Daniel *spoke forth and* blessed the God of heaven.

20.   Daniel answered and said, Blessed be the name of *the* God *of all creation,* for ever and ever. For wisdom *and glory* and might are his.

21.   And he changeth the times and the seasons. He removeth *certain* kings, and setteth up *other* kings. He giveth wisdom unto the wise, and knowledge to them that know understanding.

22.   He revealeth the deep and *the* secret things. He knoweth what *is* in the *depth of the* darkness, and the light dwelleth *up, and manifests* with him.

23.   I thank thee, and praise thee, O thou God of my fathers, who hast given me wisdom and might, and hast made known unto me now what we desired of thee. For thou hast *now* made known unto us the *secret of the* king's matter.

24.   Therefore Daniel went in unto Arioch, *the king's captain,* whom the king had ordained to destroy the wise *men* of Babylon. He went *in* and said this unto him: Destroy not the wise *men* of Babylon. Bring me in before the king, and I will show unto the king the interpretation *of his dream.*

25.   Then Arioch brought in Daniel before the king in haste, and said thus unto him, I have found a man *amongst those* of the captives of Judah, that will make known unto the king the interpretation *of his dream.*

26.   *And,* the king answered and said *un*to Daniel, whose *Babylonian* name *was* Belteshazzar, Art thou able to make known unto me *both* the dream which I have seen, and the interpretation thereof?

27.   Daniel answered in the presence of the king, and said, The secret *matter* which the king hath demanded, cannot *either* the wise *men, nor* the astrologers, *nor* the magicians, *nor* the soothsayers, *be able to* show unto the king.

28.   But there is a God in heaven that revealeth *the* secrets, and maketh *it to be* known *un*to the king, Nebuchadnezzar, what shall be *coming to pass* in the latter days. Thy dream *O king,* and the visions of thy head *which thou received as thou lay* upon thy bed, are these:

29.   As for thee, O king, thy thoughts *originally* came *into thy mind* upon thy bed, "I *wonder* what should come to pass *in the* hereafter?" And he that revealeth secrets, maketh known *un*to thee what shall come to pass.

30.   But as for me, this secret is not revealed *un*to me for *any particular* wisdom that I *may* have

more than any *other who is* living, but *actually* for *their* sakes that *were pressed, and that they* shall make known *the dream, and* the interpretation *thereof* to the king. And *in addition,* that thou, O *king,* mightest know the thoughts of thy heart.

31.   Thou, O king, sawest, and behold a great image *was presented before thee.* This great image, whose brightness *was* excellent, stood before thee; and the form thereof *was* terrible.

32.   This image's head *was made* of *a* fine gold, *and* his breast and his arms *were made* of silver, *and* his belly and his thighs *were made* of brass, *and*

33.   His legs *were made* of iron, *and* his feet *were made* part of iron and part of clay.

34.   Thou sawest *the image un*til that a stone was cut out *of a mountain* without hands, which *was used to* smote the image upon his feet, *that were* made *out* of iron and *of* clay, and brake them to pieces.

35.   Then was the iron, *and* the clay, *and* the brass, *and* the silver, and the gold, broken *in*to pieces *all* together. And *those pieces* became like the chaff of the summer threshing floors. And the wind carried them away, *so* that no place was found for them *any more.* And the stone that smote the image *into pieces,* became a great mountain, and filled *up* the whole earth.

36.   This *is* the dream *that thou hadst*; and we will *now* tell *thee of* the interpretation thereof before the king.

37.   Thou, O king, *art* a king of kings. For the God of heaven hath given *unto* thee a kingdom, *with great* power, and strength, and glory.

38.   And wheresoever the children of men dwell, the beasts of the field and the fowls of the heaven hath he given into thine hand, and hath made thee *a* ruler over them all. Thou *art* this *exalted* head of gold.

39.   And after thee *are gone, there* shall arise another kingdom *that is* inferior to thee. And *after that one is gone, yet* another third kingdom of brass, which shall *eventually* bear rule over all *of* the earth.

40.   And the fourth kingdom shall be *as* strong as iron. For as much as iron *is able to* breaketh in pieces and *then* subdueth all *things*. And as *the* iron that breaketh all *of* these *others*, shall it *also itself,* break in pieces and bruise.

41.   And whereas thou sawest the feet *of iron,* and *the* toes, part of potter's clay, and part of iron, *so* the *fifth* kingdom shall be divided. But there shall be *with*in it of the strength of the iron, forasmuch as thou sawest the iron mixed with *the* miry clay.

42.   And *as* the toes of the *iron* feet **were** part*ly* of *the* iron, and part*ly* of *the* clay, **so** the *fifth* kingdom *itself,* shall be partly strong, and partly broken.

43.   And whereas thou sawest *the* iron mixed with *the* miry clay, *so shall it be with the kings.* They shall mingle themselves with the seed of *common* men, *and attempt to acquiesce to their desires.* But they shall not cleave *strongly* one to another, *because of their attempt to please men,* even as iron is not *able to be* mixed with *miry* clay.

44.   And in the days of these kings, *which are the last days,* shall the God of heaven set up a kingdom *here on this earth,* which shall never be destroyed. And the kingdom *of his dear Son, that he shall set up* shall not be left to other people, *but* it shall break in pieces and consume all *of* these *other* kingdoms, and it shall stand for ever.

45.   Forasmuch as thou sawest that the stone was cut out of the mountain without hands, and that it brake in pieces the iron, *and* the brass, *and* the clay, *and* the silver, and the gold; *so* the great God hath made known to the king what shall come to pass hereafter. And the dream *is* certain, and the interpretation thereof *is* sure.

46.   Then the king Nebuchadnezzar fell upon his face, and worshipped Daniel, and commanded

that they should offer an oblation and sweet odours unto him.

47. The king answered unto Daniel, and said, Of a truth *it is so* that your God *is* a God of gods, and a Lord of kings, and *is* a revealer of *hidden* secrets, seeing *that* thou, *by his power,* couldest reveal this secret *of my dream.*

48. Then the king made Daniel *to be* a great man, and gave him many great gifts. And made him *to be a* ruler over the whole province of Babylon, and *the* chief of *all of* the governors *that were* over all *of* the wise *men* of Babylon.

49. Then Daniel requested of the king *on the behalf of his fellows*, and he set Shadrach, *and* Meshach, and Abednego, *to be* over the affairs of the province of Babylon. But Daniel *sat* in the gate of the king.

CHAPTER 3

1. *Then a number of years later,* Nebuchadnezzar the king made an image of gold, whose height *was* threescore cubits, *which was ninety feet high*, **and** the breadth thereof *was* six cubits, *which was nine feet wide. And* he set it up in the plain of Dura, in the province of Babylon.

2.   Then Nebuchadnezzar the king sent *his serv-ants* to gather together *all of* the princes, *and* the governors, and the captains, *and* the judges, *and* the treasurers, *and* the counsellors, *and* the sheriffs, and all *of* the rulers of the provinces, to come to the dedication of the image which Nebuchadnez-zar the king had set up.

3.   Then *all of* the princes, *and* the governors, and *the* captains, *and* the judges, *and* the treasurers, *and* the counsellors, *and* the sheriffs, and all *of* the rulers of the provinces, were gathered together unto the dedication of the image that Nebuchad-nezzar the king had set up. And they *all* stood be-fore the image that Nebuchadnezzar had set up.

4.   Then an *royal* herald cried aloud, To *all of* you it is commanded, O people, *and* nations, and languages,

5.   *That* at what time ye hear the sound of the cornet, *and the* flute, *and the* harp, *and the* sackbut, *and the* psaltery, *and the* dulcimer, and all kinds of mu-sic, *that* ye fall down and worship the golden im-age that Nebuchadnezzar the king hath set up.

6.   And whoso falleth not down and worship-peth *not,* shall the same hour be cast into the midst of a burning fiery furnace.

7.   Therefore, at that *specific* time, when all *of* the people heard the sound of the cornet, *and the* flute,

and the harp, *and the* sackbut, *and the* psaltery, and all *of the* kinds of music, all *of* the people, *and* the nations, and the languages, fell down *and* worshipped the golden image that Nebuchadnezzar the king had set up.

8.   Wherefore at that time certain Chaldeans came near *unto the king,* and accused the *captive* Jews.

9.   They spake and said to the king Nebuchadnezzar, O king, live for ever.

10.   Thou, O king, hast made a decree, that every man that shall hear the sound of the cornet, *and the* flute, *and the* harp, *and the* sackbut, *and the* psaltery, and *the* dulcimer, and all kinds of music, shall fall down and worship the golden image.

11.   And whoso falleth not down and worshippeth *that image,* *that* he should be cast into the midst of a burning fiery furnace.

12.   There are *with us* certain *captive* Jews *of influence,* whom you hast set over the affairs of the province of Babylon, *namely* Shadrach, Meshach, and Abednego. These men, O king, have not regarded thee *nor the decree that thou hast issued.* They serve not thy gods, nor *do they* worship the golden image which thou hast set up.

13.   Then Nebuchadnezzar, in *his* rage and fury *that his decree was not being followed,* commanded to

bring Shadrach, *and* Meshach, and Abednego *before him*. Then they brought these men before the king.

14.   Nebuchadnezzar spake and said unto them, *Is it* true *what I hear*, O Shadrach, Meshach, and Abednego? Do not ye serve my gods, nor *choose to* worship the golden image which I have set up?

15.   Now, if ye *shall* be ready, that at what time ye hear the sound of the cornet, *and the* flute, *and the* harp, *and the* sackbut, *and the* psaltery, and *the* dulcimer, and all kinds of music, *and* ye fall down and worship the image which I have made, *then* **well.** But if ye *choose to* worship not, ye shall be cast the same hour into the midst of a burning fiery furnace. And who *is* that God *of yours*, that shall deliver you out of my hands?

16.   Shadrach, *and* Meshach, and Abednego, answered and said *un*to the king, O Nebuchadnezzar, we **are** not *being disrespectful unto you, and shall be* careful to answer thee in this matter.

17.   If it be *so*, *that* our God whom we *worship and* serve, is able to deliver us from the burning fiery furnace, *then we rejoice* and *declare that* he will deliver *us* out of thine hand, O king.

18.   But if *that* not *be the case*, *then* be it known unto thee, O king, that we will not *in any wise* serve thy

gods, nor worship the golden image which thou hast set up.

19.   Then was Nebuchadnezzar full of *wrath and* fury, and the *appearance* form of his visage was changed against Shadrach, *and* Meshach, and Abednego. *Therefore* he spake, and commanded that they should heat the furnace *number* one, seven times more than it was *normally* wont to be heated.

20.   And he commanded *that* the most mighty *of the* men that **were** in his army *were* to bind Shadrach, *and* Meshach, and Abednego, **and** *then* to cast **them** into the burning fiery furnace.

21.   Then these *captive Jewish* men were bound *up* in their coats, *and in* their hosen, and *in* their hats, and *in* their **other** garments, and were cast into the midst of the burning fiery furnace.

22.   Therefore, because the king's commandment was *so* urgent, and the furnace *was so* exceeding*ly* hot, the flame*s* of the fire *spued forth and* slew those men that took up Shadrach, *and* Meshach, and Abednego, *to cast them into the fire.*

23.   And these three men, Shadrach, *and* Meshach, and Abednego, *then* fell down bound *up,* into the midst of the burning fiery furnace.

24.   Then Nebuchadnezzar the king was *absolutely* astonied, and rose up in haste, *and* spake, and said unto his counsellors, Did not we cast three

men bound *up* into the midst of the fire? *And* they answered and said unto the king, True, O king.

25.   He answered and said, Lo, I see four men *now* loose, *and* walking in the midst of the fire, and they *appear to* have no hurt *at all*; and the form of the fourth *man, which was the angel of the Lord,* is like *unto* the Son of God.

26.   Then Nebuchadnezzar *himself* came near to the mouth of the burning fiery furnace, *and* spake, and said, Shadrach, *and* Meshach, and Abednego, ye servants of the Most High God, *I bid thee,* come forth *out of the fire*, and come *hither.* Then Shadrach, *and* Meshach, and Abednego came forth *from out* of the midst of the *burning* fire.

27.   And the princes, *and the* governors, and *the* captains, and the king's counsellors, being gathered together saw these men, upon whose bodies the fire had no power, nor was an hair of their head *even* singed, neither were their coats *at all* changed, nor *even* the smell of *the* fire, had *not* passed *up*on them.

28.   *Then* Nebuchadnezzar spake, and said, Blessed *be* the God of Shadrach, *and* Meshach, and Abednego, who hath sent his angel, and delivered his servants *from the fiery furnace because* that *they* trusted in him. And have changed the king's word, and *have* yielded their bodies; that they

might not serve nor worship any *other* god, except their own God.

29.   Therefore I *establish and* make a decree, That *of* every people, *and* nation, and language *within my kingdom*, which *perchance may* speak any thing amiss, against the God of Shadrach, *and* Meshach, and Abednego; *that they* shall be cut in*to* pieces, and their houses shall be made a dunghill. Because there is no other God that can deliver after this sort.

30.   Then the king promoted Shadrach, *and* Meshach, and Abednego, in the province of Babylon.

CHAPTER 4

1.   *And then,* Nebuchadnezzar the king, *wrote a proclamation: Greetings* unto all *of the* people, *and* nations, and languages, that dwell in all *of* the earth; Peace be multiplied unto you.

2.   I thought it good to show *forth* the signs and *the* wonders that the *Most* High God hath wrought toward me.

3.   How great *are* his signs *indeed*! And how mighty *are* his wonders! His kingdom *is* an everlasting kingdom and his dominion *is increased* from generation to generation.

4.   I Nebuchadnezzar was at rest *with*in mine house, and *I was* flourishing *with*in my palace.

5.   *And* I saw a*nother* dream which made me *to be* afraid, and the thoughts upon my bed and the visions of my head *had* troubled me *greatly*.

6.   Therefore made I a decree to bring in all *of* the wise *men* of Babylon *once again* before me, that they might make known unto me the interpretation of the dream.

7.   Then came in *all of* the magicians, *and* the astrologers, *and* the Chaldeans, and the soothsayers. And I told *them* the dream *as I sat* before them. But they did not make known unto me the interpretation thereof.

8.   But at the last, *the Hebrew captive,* Daniel, came in before me, whose name *was* Belteshazzar, according to the name of my god, and *with*in whom *is* the spirit of the holy gods. And before him I told the dream, *saying,*

9.   O Belteshazzar, master of the magicians, because I know that the spirit of the holy gods *is* *with*in thee, and *that* no secret troubleth thee *or putteth thee off,* tell me the visions of my dream that I have seen, and the interpretation thereof.

10.   Thus *were* the visions of mine head *whilst I was* in my bed. I saw, and behold a tree *with*in the

midst of the earth, and the height *of it* thereof **was** *very* **great.**

11.   The tree grew, and *it* was strong, and the height thereof reached unto *the* heaven, and the sight thereof *was* to the end of all *of* the earth.

12.   The leaves *of the tree* thereof **were** fair, and the *abundance of the* fruit thereof *was very* much, and in it **was** *there* meat *enough* for all. The beasts of the field had *a* shadow under it, and the fowls of the heaven dwelt *with*in the boughs thereof, and all flesh was fed of it.

13.   I saw in the visions of my head *while I lay* upon my bed, and, behold, a*n angelic* watcher and an *angelic* holy one came down from heaven.

14.   He cried aloud, and said thus, "Hew down the tree, and cut off his branches. Shake off his leaves, and scatter his fruit. Let the beasts *of the field* get away from under it, and the fowls *of heaven get away* from *the protection of* his branches.

15.   Nevertheless leave the stump of his roots in the earth, even with a band of iron and *of* brass *around it, with*in the tender grass of the field. And let it be wet with the dew of *the* heaven, and *let* his portion *of meat* **be** with the beasts *of the field*, in the grass of the earth.

16.   Let his heart be changed from *a* man's *heart*, and let a beast's heart be given unto him *instead*. And let *the years* seven times pass over him."
17.   This matter *is* by the decree of the *angelic* watchers, and the demand by the word of the *other angelic* holy ones. To the intent, that the living *persons of this earth,* may know that the Most High *God* ruleth *with*in the kingdom*s* of men, and giveth it to whomsoever he will, and setteth up over it *even* the basest of men.
18.   This *is the* dream *that* I king Nebuchadnezzar have seen, *as I lay on my bed.* Now thou, O Belteshazzar, declare *unto me* the interpretation *of the dream* thereof, forasmuch as all *of* the wise men of my kingdom are not able to make *it* known unto me *concerning* the interpretation. But thou art able, for *I perceive that* the spirit of the holy gods is in thee.
19.   Then Daniel, whose *Babylonian* name *was* Belteshazzar, was *surprisingly* astonied for *about* one hour, and his thoughts troubled him *greatly.* The king spake, and said *unto him,* Belteshazzar, let not the dream or the interpretation thereof, trouble thee. *And* Belteshazzar answered and said, My lord, the dream *be favorable* to them that hate thee, and the interpretation thereof *also favorable* to thine enemies.

20.   The tree that thou sawest, which grew, and
was strong, whose height reached unto the heaven,
and the sight thereof *in*to all *of* the earth,
21.   Whose leaves *were* fair, and the *abundant*
fruit thereof *was* much, and in it *was there* meat for
all *to eat*. Under which the beasts of the field dwelt,
and upon whose branches the fowls of the heaven
had their habitation.
22.   It *is* thou, O king *that is that very tree*, that art
grown and become strong. For thy greatness is
grown, and reacheth unto *the* heaven, and thy dominion *reacheth* to the end of *all of* the earth.
23.   And whereas the king saw a*n angelic* watcher
and an *other angelic* holy one coming down from
heaven, and saying, "Hew the tree down, and destroy it. Yet leave the stump of the roots thereof in
the earth, even with a band of iron and *of* brass
around it, *with*in the tender grass of the field. And
because of the insanity that shall come upon thee, let it be wet
with the dew of *the* heaven, and *let* his portion *of*
meat be with the beasts of the field till *the years* sev-
en times pass over him."
24.   This *is* the interpretation, O king. And this
is the decree *put forth* of the Most High *God*, which
is *now* come upon my lord the king:
25.   That they *that* shall *preserve thee, shall* drive thee
away from men, *so that thine enemies shall not kill thee.*

And *because of thine insanity,* thy dwelling shall be with the beasts of the field, and they shall make thee to eat grass as *the* oxen, and they shall wet thee with the dew of heaven, and *the years* seven times shall pass over thee, till thou *shalt recover from thine insanity, and* know that the Most High *God* ruleth in the kingdom of men, and giveth it to whomsoever he will.

26.   And whereas they commanded to leave the stump of the tree roots; thy kingdom shall be sure unto thee, *and shall not be taken away from thee,* after that thou shalt have *returned unto thy sanity, and* known that the heavens do rule.

27.   Wherefore, O king, *I beseech thee,* let my counsel be *heard, and let it be* acceptable unto thee, and *choose to* break off *from* thy sins by *turning unto* righteousness, and thine iniquities *shall be forgiven unto thee* by shewing mercy to the poor. If *perchance,* it may be a lengthening of thy *days of* tranquility.

28.   *However,* all *of* this *still* came upon the king Nebuchadnezzar.

29.   *So,* at the end of twelve months *of grace,* he walked *with*in the palace of the kingdom of Babylon.

30.   The king spake, and said, Is not this great city *of* Babylon, that I have built for *the purpose of being* the house *of renown,* of the *whole* kingdom, by the *very*

might of my *own* power, and for the honour of my *personal* majesty, *wonderful?*

31. *And,* while the word *was still within* the king's mouth, there fell a voice from heaven, *saying,* "O king Nebuchadnezzar, to thee it is *thus* spoken; The kingdom *is now* departed from thee.

32. And they *that shall preserve thee,* shall *come and* drive thee *away* from men, *so that thine enemies shall not kill thee.* And thy dwelling *shall be* with the beasts of the field. *And* they shall make thee to eat grass as *the* oxen, and *the years* seven times shall pass over thee, until thou *shalt* know that the Most High *God* ruleth in the kingdom of men, and giveth it to whomsoever he will."

33. The same hour was the *very* thing fulfilled upon Nebuchadnezzar. And he was driven *away* from men *for his own safety,* and did eat grass as *the* oxen, and his body was wet with the dew of heaven, till his hairs were grown *out* like eagles' *feathers,* and his nails *were* like *unto* bird's *claws.*

34. And at the end of the *seven years of* days, I Nebuchadnezzar lifted up mine eyes unto *the* heaven, and mine understanding returned unto me *just as it was declared,* and I blessed the Most High *God.* And I praised and honoured him that liveth for ever *and ever,* whose dominion *is* an everlasting

dominion, and his kingdom *is* from generation to generation.

35.   And all *of* the inhabitants of the earth *are* reputed as *being* nothing *compared to him.* And he doeth according to his *own* will in the army of heaven, and *among* the inhabitants of the earth. And none can stay his hand, or say unto him, What doest thou?

36.   At the same time, my reason returned unto me *even as it was declared.* And for the glory of my kingdom, mine honour and *my* brightness *was* returned unto me. And my counsellors and my lords sought unto me *for counsel.* And I was established in my kingdom *once again,* and excellent majesty was added unto me.

37.   Now I Nebuchadnezzar praise and extol and honour the King of heaven, all *of* whose works *are* truth, and his ways *are the ways of* judgment. And those that *continue to* walk in pride, he is able to abase.

CHAPTER 5

1.   *As time went on,* Belshazzar the king, *who was the grand-son of king Nebuchadnezzar, and co-regent with his father, king Nabonidus,* made a great feast to a thousand of his lords, *while his father went to meet king Cyrus*

in battle, and *he* drank wine before the thousand *lords.*

2.   *And,* Belshazzar, whiles he tasted *of* the wine, commanded *for* to bring the golden and silver vessels which his *grand-*father Nebuchadnezzar had taken out of the temple *of the living God,* which *was* in Jerusalem; *so* that the king, and his princes, *and* his wives, and his concubines, might *be able to* drink therein *at their feast.*

3.   Then they brought the golden vessels, that were taken out of the temple of the house of *the Most High* God, which *was* at Jerusalem; and the king, and his princes, *and* his wives, and his concubines, drank *their wine* in them.

4.   They drank *their* wine, and praised the gods of gold, and of silver, *and* of brass, *and* of iron, *and* of wood, and of stone.

5.   In the same hour *of the night* came forth fingers, *as* of a man's hand, and wrote *on the wall,* over against the candlestick, upon the plaster of the wall of the king's palace. And the king *visibly* saw the part of the hand that wrote.

6.   Then the king's *facial* countenance was *suddenly* changed. And his thoughts troubled him *greatly,* so that the joints of his loins were loos*e*ned, and his knees smote one against another *in abject fear.*

7.   The king *then* cried aloud to *quickly* bring in the astrologers, *and* the Chaldeans, and the soothsayers. *And* the king spake, and said to the wise *men* of Babylon, Whosoever shall read this writing *that is on the wall*, and shew *unto* me the interpretation thereof, shall be clothed with *expensive* scarlet, and *have* a chain of gold *placed* about his neck, and shall be*come* the third ruler in the kingdom.

8.   Then came in all *of* the king's wise *men*. But they could not read the writing *on the wall*, nor make *it* known *un*to the king *concerning* the interpretation thereof.

9.   Then was king Belshazzar greatly troubled, and his *facial* countenance was *again radically* changed in him, and his lords were astonied *at the sight*.

10.   *Now* the queen, by reason of the words of the king and *of* his lords, came into the banquet house. *And* the queen spake and said, O king, live for ever. Let not thy thoughts *continue to* trouble thee, nor let thy countenance be *radically* changed.

11.   There is a man O *king*, in thy kingdom, in whom *is* the spirit of the holy gods. And in the days of thy *grand*-father, light and understanding and wisdom, like the wisdom of the gods, was found in him. *To* whom the king Nebuchadnezzar, thy *grand-*

father, made master of the magicians, *and the* astrologers, *and the* Chaldeans, *and the* soothsayers.

12.   Forasmuch as an excellent spirit, and *heavenly* knowledge, and *good* understanding, *and the* interpreting of dreams, and *the* shewing *forth* of the hard sentences, and *the* dissolving of *the* doubts, were found in the same *Hebrew captive* Daniel, whom the king named Belteshazzar. Now let Daniel be called, and he will shew *unto the king* the interpretation *thereof.*

13.   Then was Daniel *sent for, and* brought in before the king. *And* the king spake and said unto Daniel, *Art* thou that Daniel, which *art* of the *Israeli* children of the captivity of Judah, whom the *former* king, my *grand-*father, brought out of Jewry?

14.   I have even heard of thee, that the spirit of the *holy* gods *is* in thee, and *that* light and understanding and excellent wisdom is found *with*in thee.

15.   And now the wise *men, and* the astrologers, have been brought in before me, that they should read this writing *that is on the wall,* and make known unto me the interpretation thereof. But they could not shew *unto me* the interpretation of the thing.

16.   And I have heard of thee, that thou canst make interpretations *known,* and dissolve doubts. Now if thou canst read the writing, and make

known *unto* me the interpretation thereof, thou shalt be clothed with *expensive* scarlet, and *have* a chain of gold *placed* about thy neck, and shalt be *installed as* the third ruler in the kingdom.

17.   Then Daniel answered and said before the king, Let thy gifts be *kept unto* thyself O *king*, and give thy rewards *unto* another. Yet I will read the writing unto the king, and make known *unto* him the interpretation.

18.   O thou king, the Most High God gave *unto* Nebuchadnezzar thy *grand*-father a *magnificent* kingdom, and *afforded him* majesty, and glory, and honour.

19.   And for the majesty that he gave *unto* him, all *of the* people, *and the* nations, and *the* languages, trembled and feared before him. *And* whom he would *choose,* he slew. And whom he would *choose,* he kept alive. And whom he would *choose,* he set up. And whom he would *choose,* he put down.

20.   But when his heart was lifted up, and his mind *was* hardened in pride, he was deposed from his kingly throne, and they took his glory from him.

21.   And he was driven from the sons of men *for his own safety*. And his heart was made like *unto* the beasts, and his dwelling *was* with the wild asses. They fed him with grass like *the* oxen, and his

body was wet with the dew of heaven; *un*til he knew that the Most High God ruled in the kingdom of men, and *that* he appointed over it whomsoever he will.

22.   And *now,* thou his *grand*-son, O Belshazzar, hast not *at all* humbled thine heart *before the Lord God Almighty*, *even* though thou knowest all *of* this *that I have shared with thee.*

23.   But *thou* hast lifted up thyself against the Lord of heaven. And they, *thy servants,* have brought *in* the *sanctified* vessels of his house before thee, and thou and thy lords, *and* thy wives, and thy concubines, have *all mocked God, and* drunk wine in them. And *then* thou hast praised the gods of silver, and *of* gold, *and* of brass, *and of* iron, *and of* wood, and *of* stone, which *neither* see not, nor *do they* hear, nor *do they* know *anything at all.* And the God in whose hand thy breath *really is*, and *to* whose, *are* all *of* thy ways *attributed*, hast thou not glorified *at all.*

24.   Then was the part of the hand *once again* sent from him *and seen*; and this writing was written.

25.   And this *is* the writing that was written, MENE, MENE, TEKEL, UPHARSIN.

26.   This *is now* the interpretation of the thing O *king*: MENE; God hath numbered *the days of* thy kingdom, and *hath* finished it.

27. TEKEL; Thou art weighed in the balances *thyself*, and are found wanting.

28. PERES; Thy kingdom is *now* divided, and *is* given to the Medes and *the* Persians.

29. Then commanded Belshazzar *unto his men*, and they clothed Daniel with *expensive* scarlet, and *put* a chain of gold about his neck, and made a *public* proclamation concerning him, that he should be*come* the third ruler in the kingdom.

30. *And* in that *very* night was Belshazzar the king of the Chaldeans slain.

31. And Darius the Median took *up* the kingdom, *being* about *sixty-two, or* threescore and two years old.

CHAPTER 6

1. *And,* it pleased Darius to set over the kingdom an hundred and twenty princes, which should be over the whole *of the* kingdom.

2. And over these *one-hundred and twenty princes*, *there were* three presidents *that were then installed*; of whom Daniel *was to be the* first. That the princes might give accounts unto them, and the king should have no damage *to his credibility*.

3. Then this Daniel, was preferred above the *other* presidents and *all of the* princes, because *of* an

excellent spirit *that was* in him; and the king *actually* thought to set him over the whole realm.

4.   Then the *other* presidents and *all of the* princes sought to find *an* occasion *to come* against Daniel concerning the kingdom. But they could find none occasion nor fault *in what Daniel did*; forasmuch as he *was* faithful, *and* neither was there any error or fault found in him.

5.   Then said these men *because of their jealousy*, We shall not find any occasion *to come* against this Daniel, except we find *it* against him concerning the law of his God.

6.   Then these *other* presidents and *all of the* princes assembled *themselves* together, *and went un*to the king, and said thus unto him, O King Darius, live for ever.

7.   All *of* the presidents of the kingdom, *and* the governors, and the princes, *and* counsellors, and the captains, have consulted together to establish a royal statute, and to make a firm decree, that whosoever shall ask a petition of any God or *of any* man for thirty days, save of thee *only*, O king, he shall be cast into the den of lions.

8.   Now, O king, establish the decree *that we have all agreed upon*, and sign the writing *of it*, that it be not changed, according to the law of the Medes and *the* Persians, which altereth not.

9.   Wherefore king Darius signed the writing and *established* the decree.

10.   Now when Daniel knew that the writing was signed, he went into his house *to pray*. And his windows being open in his chamber, *facing* toward Jerusalem, he kneeled *down* upon his knees *openly* three times a day, and prayed, and gave thanks before his God, as he did aforetime.

11.   Then these men assembled *secretly*, and found Daniel praying and making supplication before his God.

12.   Then they came near, and spake before the king concerning the king's decree. *And they asked of the king,* Hast thou not signed a decree, that every man that shall ask a *petition* of any God or *of any* man within thirty days, save of thee *only*, O king, shall be cast into the den of lions? The*n the* king answered *unto them* and said, The thing *is* true, according to the law of the Medes and *the* Persians, which altereth not.

13.   Then answered they and said before the king, *O king, live for ever,* that *Hebrew* Daniel, which *is* of the *Israeli* children of the captivity of Judah, regardeth not thee, O king, nor the decree that thou has signed, but maketh his petition three times a day *unto his God*.

14.   Then the king, when he heard *these* words, was *repentant, and* sore displeased with himself *because of the decree that he had established*, and *he* set *his* heart *to move* on Daniel's *behalf,* to deliver him. And he labored *all the day long un*til the going down of the sun to *find some way to* deliver him.

15.   Then these *wicked* men assembled *themselves* unto the king, and said unto the king, Know *thou this,* O king, that the law of the Medes and *the* Persians *is now,* That no decree nor statute which the king establisheth may be changed.

16.   Then the king commanded *accordingly,* and they brought Daniel *unto the place,* and *they straightway* cast *him* into the den of *the* lions. *Now* the king spake and said unto Daniel, *Be encouraged O Daniel, for I believe that* thy God whom thou servest continually; *that* he will deliver thee.

17.   And a stone was brought, and laid upon the mouth of the *lion's* den *so that Daniel could not climb out.* And the king *personally* sealed it with his own signet *ring,* and with the signet *rings* of his lords; *so* that the purpose *of putting him into the den of lions* might not be changed concerning Daniel.

18.   Then the king went *in*to his palace, and passed the night fasting. Neither were instruments of musick brought before him *for comfort.* And his sleep went from him.

19.   Then the king arose very early in the morning, and went in haste unto the den of *the* lions.

20.   And when he *finally* came *un*to the den, he cried with a lamentable voice unto Daniel. *And* the king spake and said to Daniel, O Daniel, servant of the living God, is thy God, whom thou servest continually, able to deliver thee from the lions?

21.   Then said Daniel unto the king, O king, live for ever.

22.   My God hath sent *unto me* his angel, and hath shut the lion's mouths, that they have not hurt me. Forasmuch as before him innocency was found in me; and also before thee, O king, have I done no hurt.

23.   Then was the king exceeding glad for him, and *happily* commanded that they should take Daniel up *and* out of the den *of the lions*. So Daniel was taken up *and* out of the den, and no manner of hurt was found upon him, because he believed in his God *to deliver him*.

24.   And the king *immediately* commanded, and they brought those *wicked* men which had accused Daniel, and they cast *them* into the den of *the* lions. Them, *and* their children, and their wives, *were cast into the den*. And the lions had the mastery of

them, and brake all their bones in pieces *before* ever they *even* came *to be* at the bottom of the den.

25.   Then king Darius wrote *a proclamation* unto all *of the* people, *and the* nations, and *the* languages, that dwell in all *of* the earth: Peace be multiplied unto you.

26.   I *king Darius* make a decree, That in every dominion of my kingdom *should* men tremble and fear before the God of Daniel. For he *is* the living God, and *remains* stedfast for ever, and his kingdom *is of that* which shall not be destroyed, and his dominion *shall be even* unto the end *of time.*

27.   He delivereth and rescueth *whomsoever he will,* and he worketh signs and wonders in heaven and in *the* earth *beneath*; who hath delivered *his servant* Daniel from the power of the lions.

28.   So this *Hebrew captive* Daniel prospered *with*in the reign of *king* Darius, and *with*in the reign of *king* Cyrus the Persian.

CHAPTER 7

1.   *Previously, with*in the first year of *the reign of* Belshazzar, *the* king of Babylon, *who was the grandson of king Nebuchadnezzar, and the co-regent son of Nabonidus*; *the Hebrew captive* Daniel had a dream, and visions of his head *while he was laying* upon his bed. Then he

wrote *down* the dream *and* told *forth* the sum of the matters.

2.   Daniel spake and said, I saw in my vision by *the* night, and, behold, the four winds of the heaven, *representing the four consecutive kingdoms of the great image that Nebuchadnezzar saw,* strove upon the great sea *of the peoples of the earth.*

3.   And four great beasts, *representing the four varied kingdoms,* came up from the sea *of the peoples of the earth, and they were* diverse one from another.

4.   The first *beastly kingdom* **was** like *that of* a lion *and represents the Babylonian Empire,* and *it* had eagle's wings *that represents that it conquered quickly.* I beheld till the wings thereof were plucked *from him,* and it was lifted up from the earth, and made *to* stand upon the feet as a man *because of Nebuchadnezzar's insanity,* and a man's heart was given to it.

5.   And behold another beast *arose,* a second, like *un*to a bear *representing the Medo-Persian Empire,* and it raised up itself on *the* one side, *as Cyrus was a stronger ruler than Darius,* and ***it had*** three ribs in the mouth of it between the teeth of it *representing conquered Babylon, and Lydia, and Egypt.* And they said thus unto it, Arise, *and* devour much flesh.

6.   After this I beheld, and lo another *beast arose,* like *un*to a leopard *representing the Grecian Empire,* which had upon the back of it four wings of a

fowl, *representing the increased swiftness of its conquering.* The beast had also four heads, *representing the four divisions that the Empire was to be broken up into*; and dominion was given *unto* it.

7.   After this I saw in the night visions, and behold a fourth beast *arose, representing the Roman Empire. And it was* dreadful and terrible, and strong exceedingly. And it had great iron teeth *representing its fierceness.* It devoured and brake in*to* pieces, and stamped *even* the residue *that was left* with the feet of it. And it *was* diverse from all *of* the *other* beasts that **were** before it. And it had ten horns *representing the ten kingdoms that shall come together in the latter days.*

8.   I considered the *ten* horns *which represent ten countries of the Old Roman Empire in the latter days*, and, behold, there came up among them another little horn *which represents one of the countries, and the leader of that country, who will become the Anitchrist.* Before whom there were three of the first horns, *or countries, which were* plucked up by the roots *because of military defeat.* And, behold, in this *little* horn **were** eyes like the eyes of *a* man, and a mouth speaking great things.

9.   I beheld *until all of* the thrones were cast down *representing the rebellious countries*, and the Ancient of Days did sit *upon his throne*, whose garment **was** white as snow, and the hair of his head like the pure wool. His throne **was** *like* the fiery flame,

and his wheels *as* burning fire, *and he cast the rebellious of the countries into Hell.*

10.   A fiery stream *of judgment from a Great White Throne,* issued and came forth from before him. Thousands *and* thousands ministered unto him, and ten thousand times ten thousand stood before him. The judgment was set, and the books were opened.

11.   I beheld then, because of the voice of the great words which the *little* horn spake. I beheld *even un*til the beast *known of as the Antichrist* was slain, and his body destroyed, and given *un*to the burning flame.

12.   As concerning the rest of the *four* beasts, they had their dominion taken away. Yet their lives were prolonged for a season and *a* time *until they each were succeeded by another.*

13.   I saw in the night visions, and, behold, *one* like *unto* the Son of man, *whose name was Jesus,* came with clouds of heaven, and came to the Ancient of Days *who is his Father,* and they brought him near before him.

14.   And there was given *unto* him dominion, and glory, and a kingdom, that all *of the* people, *and all of the* nations, and *the various* languages, should serve him. His dominion *is* an everlasting dominion,

which shall not *ever* pass away, and his kingdom *is* *that* which shall not be destroyed.

15.   I Daniel was grieved in my spirit in the midst of *my* body, and the visions of my head troubled me.

16.   I came near unto one of them that stood by *me, named Gabriel,* and asked him the truth of all *of* this. So he told me, and made me *to* know *of* the interpretation of the things.

17.   These great beasts, which are four *in number, are* four kings, *which* shall arise out of the earth.

18.   But *in the latter days,* the saints of the Most High *God* shall take the Kingdom *of Heaven,* and possess the kingdom for ever, even for ever and ever.

19.   Then I would know the truth of the fourth beast *representing the Roman Empire,* which was diverse from all *of* the others. *He was* exceeding dreadful, whose teeth *were made of* iron, and his nails, *were claws of* brass. *Which* devoured, *and* brake in pieces, and stamped *out* the residue *of the other kingdoms* with his feet.

20.   And of *all of* the ten horns that *were* in his head, and *of* the other*s* which came up, and be-fore whom *the* three fell; even *of* that *one* horn*, he* that had eyes, and a mouth that spake very great

swelling things, whose look *was* more stout than his fellows.

21.   I beheld, and the same horn *in the latter days* made war with the *New Creation* saints *of God*, and prevailed against them.

22.   Until the Ancient of Days came *in the latter days*, and judgment was given *un*to the *New Creation* saints of the Most High *God, during the Millennial Reign of Christ*. And the time came that the *New Creation* saints possessed the Kingdom *of Heaven*.

23.   Thus he said, The fourth beast shall be the fourth kingdom upon the earth, which shall be diverse from all *of the other* kingdoms, and shall devour the whole *known* earth, and shall tread it down, and break it in*to* pieces *during the days of the Roman Empire*.

24.   And the ten horns *that shall come* out of this kingdom, *which is the Revised Roman Empire, are the* ten kings *that* shall arise *in the latter days*. And another *king* shall rise after them. And he shall be diverse from the first, and he shall subdue three kings *through military combat*.

25.   And *as the Antichrist,* he shall speak *great* swelling words against the Most High *God*, and shall wear out the *New Creation* saints of the Most High *God*, and think to change *the* times and *the* laws. And they shall be given into his hand until a time,

and times, and the dividing of *a* time, *or three and one-half years.*

26. But the judgment *of God* shall sit, and they shall *ultimately* take away his dominion, *and his ambition,* to consume and to destroy *it* unto the end.

27. And the Kingdom *of Heaven,* and dominion, and the greatness of the kingdom under the whole *of the* heaven, shall be given *un*to the people of the *New Creation* saints of the Most High *God, and to his Christ,* whose kingdom *is* an everlasting kingdom, and all *of the* dominions shall serve *Christ Jesus* and obey him.

28. Hitherto *is* the end of the matter. As for me Daniel, my cognitions much troubled me *in my heart,* and my countenance changed *with*in me: but I kept the matter in my heart.

CHAPTER 8

1. In the third year of the reign of king Belshazzar a*nother* vision appeared unto me, *even unto* me Daniel, after that *one* which appeared unto me at the first.

2. And I saw in a vision; and it came to pass, when I saw, that I *was* at Shushan *with*in the palace, which *is* in the province of Elam; and I saw in a vision, and I was by the river of Ulai.

3.   Then I lifted up mine eyes, and saw, and behold, there stood before the river a ram which had *two* horns *which were the kings of Media and Persia.* And the *two* horns *were* high; but *the* one *which was Persia, was* higher than the other, and the higher *one* came up last.

4.   I saw the ram pushing westward *to conquer Lydia,* and northward *to conquer Babylon,* and south-ward *to conquer Egypt;* so that no beasts might stand before him, neither *was there any* that could de-liver out of his hand. But he did according to *all of* his will, and became great.

5.   And as I was considering, behold, an he goat came from *the country of Greece on* the west, *and went conquering* on the face of the whole earth, and touched not the ground. And the goat *had* a nota-ble horn between his eyes, *who was known of as Alex-ander the Great.*

6.   And he came to the ram that had *two* horns, which I had seen standing before the river, and ran into him in the fury of his power *because of the hatred that the Greeks had against the Medo-Persian Empire.*

7.   And I saw him come close unto the ram, and he was moved with choler against him, and *he* smote the ram, and brake his two horns. And there was no power in the ram to stand *in defense* before him, but he cast him down to the ground,

and stamped upon him. And there was none that could deliver the ram out of his hand.

8.   Therefore the he goat waxed very great. And when he was *yet* strong, the great horn *named Alexander the Great* was broken. And for it came up *the* four notable ones, *which were his four generals,* toward the four winds of heaven.

9.   And out of one of them came forth *in the latter days,* a little horn *which is the Antichrist, and* which waxed exceeding great, toward the south *which is Egypt,* and toward the east *which is Iraq,* and toward the pleasant *land which is Israel.*

10.   And it waxed great, *even un*to the *Hebrew priest* host of heaven. And it cast down *some* of the *Hebrew priest* host and *some* of the *Hebrew worshipping* stars to the ground, and stamped upon them.

11.   Yea, he magnified *himself* even *un*to the prince of the *Hebrew priest* host, *which is the High Priest of Israel,* and by him the daily *animal* sacrifice was taken away, and the place of his *temple* sanctuary was cast down.

12.   And an host *of those abounding in sin,* was given *unto* **him** against the daily *animal* **sacrifice** by reason of transgression, and it cast down the truth to the ground. And it practiced *wickedness,* and prospered.

13.   Then I heard one *New Creation* saint speaking, and another *New Creation* saint said unto that certain *New Creation* **saint** which spake, How long **shall be** the vision *concerning* the daily *sacrifice*, and the transgression of *the abomination of* desolation, to give both the sanctuary and the *Hebrew worshipping* host, to be trodden under foot?
14.   And he said unto me, Unto two thousand and three hundred days; *and* then shall the sanctuary be cleansed.
15.   And it came to pass, when I, *even* I Daniel, had seen the vision, and sought for the meaning, then, behold, there stood before me *an angel,* as the appearance of a man.
16.   And I heard a man's voice between *the banks of* Ulai, which called, and said, Gabriel, make this *man* to understand the vision.
17.   So he came near *to* where I stood. And when he came, I was afraid, and fell *down* upon my face. But he said unto me, Understand, O son of man. For *in the latter days,* at the time of the end **shall be** the vision.
18.   Now as he was speaking with me, I was *suddenly* in a deep sleep on my face toward the ground. But he touched me *gently*, and set me upright *on my feet.*

19.   And he said, Behold, I will make thee *to* know what shall be *coming* in the last end of the indignation. For at the time appointed, *of the Second Coming of Christ Jesus,* the end *shall be.*

20.   The ram which thou sawest having *two* horns *are* the kings of Media and Persia.

21.   And the rough *he*-goat *is* the king of Grecia. And the great horn that *is* between his eyes *is* the first king *who is Alexander the Great.*

22.   Now that *king* being broken, whereas four *of his generals* stood up for it. Four *separate* kingdoms shall stand up out of the Nation *of Greece,* but not *with*in his *family* power.

23.   And in the latter time of their kingdom, when the transgressors are come to the full, *the Antichrist,* a king of fierce countenance, and understanding dark sentences, shall stand up.

24.   And his power shall be mighty, but not *just* by his own power. And he shall destroy wonderfully, and shall prosper, and *shall* practice *wickedness,* and shall destroy the mighty and the holy people *of God.*

25.   And through his policy also he shall cause craft to prosper in his hand. And he shall magnify *himself with*in his *own* heart, and by peace shall *he* destroy many. He shall also stand up against *Jesus*

Christ, who is the **Prince of princes. But he shall** *ultimately* **be broken,** *and that* **without hand.**

26.   **And the vision of the evening and the morning which was told** *unto thee is* **true. Wherefore shut thou up the vision** *that thou hast seen.* **For it** *shall not be fulfilled* **for many days.**

27.   **And I Daniel fainted, and was sick** *certain* **days. Afterward I rose up, and did the king's business. And I was astonished at the vision, but none** *other man* **understood** *it.*

CHAPTER 9

1.   **In the first year of** *king* **Darius, the son of** *king* **Ahasuerus,** *who is really named Xerxes,* **of the seed of the Medes, which was made** *to be the* **king over the realm of the Chaldeans.**

2.   **In the first year of his reign, I Daniel understood by** *the* **books** *that had been kept,* **the number of the years** *of captivity,* **whereof the word of the Lord came** *un*t**o Jeremiah the prophet, that he would accomplish seventy years in the desolations of Jerusalem.**

3.   **And I set my face unto the Lord God, to seek** *understanding,* **by prayer and supplications, with fasting, and sackcloth, and ashes.**

4.   And I prayed unto the Lord my God, and made my confession, and said, O Lord, the great and dreadful God, keeping the covenant *always* and *rendering* mercy to them that love him, and to them that keep his commandments.

5.   We have sinned *O Lord*, and have committed iniquity, and have done wickedly, and have rebelled, even by *our* departing from thy precepts and from thy judgments.

6.   Neither have we hearkened unto thy servants the prophets *who were your spokesmen*, which spake in thy name to our kings, *and to* our princes, and *to* our fathers, and to all *of* the people of the land.

7.   O Lord, righteousness *belongeth* unto thee, but unto us confusion of faces, as at this day *because of our disobedience*. To the men of Judah, and to the inhabitants of Jerusalem, and unto all *of* Israel *that are* near, and *that are* afar off, through all *of* the countries whither thou hast driven them, because of their trespass that they have trespassed against thee.

8.   O Lord, to us *belongeth* confusion of face *because of our disobedience*, to our kings, *and* to our princes, and to our fathers, because we have *grievously* sinned against thee.

9.   To the Lord our God *belong* mercies and forgiveness, *even* though we have rebelled against him.

10.   Neither have we obeyed the voice of the Lord our God, to walk in *all of* his laws, which he set before us by his servants the prophets.

11.   Yea, all *of* Israel have transgressed thy law, even by departing *from thee*, that they might not obey thy voice. Therefore the curse *that is written* is poured upon us, and the oath that *is* written in the Law of Moses the servant of God, because we have sinned against him.

12.   And he hath confirmed his words, which he spake against us, and against our judges that judged us, by bringing upon us a great evil. For under the whole *of* heaven *there* hath not been done *ought,* as hath been done upon Jerusalem.

13.   As *it is* written *with*in the Law of Moses, *within the Book of Deuteronomy,* all *of* this evil is come upon us. Yet made we not our prayer *of repentance* before the Lord our God, that we might turn from our iniquities, and understand thy truth.

14.   Therefore hath the Lord watched upon the evil, and brought it upon us *as the Law of Moses decrees.* For the Lord our God *is* righteous in all *of* his works which he doeth. For we obeyed not his voice.

15.　And now, O Lord our God, that hast brought thy people forth out of the land of Egypt with a mighty hand, and hast gotten thee renown, we *declare that we* have done wickedly.

16.　O Lord, according to all *of* thy righteousness, I beseech thee, let thine anger and thy fury be turned away for thy city Jerusalem, thy holy mountain*'s sake.* Because for our sins, and for the iniquities of our fathers, Jerusalem and thy people *are become* a reproach to all *of the nations* **that are** *round* about us.

17.　Now therefore, O our God, hear the prayer of thy servant and his supplications, and cause thy face to shine upon thy sanctuary that is desolate, for the Lord's sake.

18.　O my God, incline thine ear, and hear. Open thine eyes, and behold our desolations, and the city which is called by thy name. For we do not present our supplications before thee for our *own* righteousness *sake,* but for thy great mercies.

19.　O Lord, hear. O Lord, forgive. O Lord, hearken and do. Defer not, for thine own sake, O my God. For thy city and thy people are called by thy *holy* name.

20.　And whiles I *was* speaking, and praying, and confessing my sin and the sin of my people Israel, and presenting my supplication before the

Lord my God, for the holy mountain of my God *which is the city of Jerusalem*;

21.   Yea, whiles I *was* speaking in prayer, even the man-*like, angel* Gabriel, whom I had seen in the vision at the beginning, being caused to fly swiftly, touched me about the time of the evening oblation.

22.   And he informed *me*, and talked with me, and said, O Daniel, I am now come forth to give thee skill and understanding.

23.   At the *very* beginning of thy supplications, the commandment came forth *from the throne*, and I am *now* come to shew *thee*. For thou *art* greatly beloved. Therefore understand the matter, and consider the vision.

24.   Seventy weeks, *which is really four-hundred and ninety years* are determined *from heaven, as a set time for judgment*, upon thy people and upon thy holy city, to finish *and to bring to an end*, the transgression; and to make an *complete and definitive* end of *thy* sins; and to make *eternal* reconciliation of iniquity; and to *finally* bring in everlasting righteousness; and to seal up the *totality of the* vision and prophecy *concerning thy Nation of Israel*; and to *cleanse and* anoint the most Holy *of Holies sanctuary which is within the temple, and the city, of Jerusalem.*

25.   Know therefore and understand, *that* from the going forth of the *third* commandment *that is*

given to **restore and to** *re*build **Jerusalem***, which was in the twentieth year of the reign of Artaxerxes,* **unto the Messiah the Prince** *shall be* **seven weeks, and threescore and two weeks,** *which is four-hundred and eighty-three years.* **The street***s of Jerusalem* **shall be built again, and the wall, even in troublous times** *within the days of the prophet Nehemiah.*
26. **And after** *the completion of the building, which will take forty-nine years,* *then* **threescore and two weeks** *later, which is four-hundred and thirty-four years,* **shall Messiah be cut off** *by crucifixion,* **but not for Himself. And the** *Roman Empire* **people of the prince that shall come, shall destroy the city** *of Jerusalem,* **and the sanctuary** *of thy holy temple.* **And the end thereof** *shall be* **with a flood** *of destructions,* **and** *even* **unto the end of the war** *with Antichrist,* **desolations are determined.**
27. **And he,** *that is the Antichrist,* **shall confirm the** *latter days* **covenant** *of peace* **with many** *within the Nation of Israel,* **for one week,** *which is seven years.* **And in the midst of the** *one* **week he shall cause the** *animal* **sacrifice and the** *worship* **oblation to cease. And for the overspreading of abomination***s of self-exaltation,* **he shall make** *it* **desolate, even until the consummation** *of the seventieth week.* **And that** *being* **determined,** *destruction for Antichrist* **shall be poured** *forth* **upon the desolate.**

CHAPTER 10

1.   In the third year of Cyrus, *the* king of Persia, a thing was revealed unto Daniel, whose name was called Belteshazzar *in the Babylonian language.* And the thing *was* true, but the time appointed *for fulfillment was* long. And he understood the thing, and had understanding of the vision.

2.   In those days I Daniel was *in* mourning *for* three full weeks.

3.   I ate no pleasant bread, neither came *any* flesh nor wine in*to* my mouth, neither did I anoint myself at all *during the interim of time,* un*til* three whole weeks were fulfilled.

4.   And in the four and twentieth day of the first month, *which is called Abib,* as I was by the side of the great river, which *is called* Hiddekel,

5.   Then I lifted up mine eyes, and looked, and behold a certain man, *which was the Angel of the Lord,* clothed in linen, whose loins *were* girded with *the* fine gold of Uphaz.

6.   His body also *was* like *unto* the beryl *stone,* and his face *was* as the appearance of lightning, and his eyes *were* as lamps of fire, and his arms and his feet *were* like in colour to polished brass, and the voice of his words *was* like the voice of a multitude.

7.   And I Daniel alone saw the vision. For the men that were with me saw not the vision. But a great quaking fell upon them *as they perceived me*, so that they fled to hide themselves.

8.   Therefore I was left alone, and saw this great vision, and there remained no strength in me *at all*. For my comeliness was turned *with*in me into corruption, and I retained no strength *at all*.

9.   Yet heard I the voice of his words. And when I heard the voice of his words, then *immediately* was I in a deep sleep on my face, and my face *was* toward the ground.

10.   And, behold, an hand touched me, which *did* set me *up* upon my knees and *upon* the palms of my hands.

11.   And he said unto me, O Daniel, a man greatly beloved, understand the words that I *now* speak unto thee, and stand upright *upon thy feet*. For unto thee am I now sent *from before the face of the Lord*. And when he had spoken this word unto me, I stood trembling.

12.   Then said he unto me, Fear not, Daniel, for from the *very* first day that thou didst set thine heart to *repent, and to* understand, and to chasten thyself before thy God, thy words were heard, and I am come for thy words.

13.   But the *unholy, overseeing* prince of the kingdom of Persia withstood me *in my coming unto thee,*
one and twenty days. But, lo, Michael, one of the
chief princes, *and the overseer of your Nation of Israel*,
came to help me. And *still*, I remained there *for a
time* with the kings of Persia.

14.   Now I am come *unto thee*, to make thee understand what shall befall thy people in the latter
days. For yet the vision *is not scheduled to actually occur
for many* days.

15.   And when he had spoken such words unto
me, I set my face *once again* toward the ground, and
I became dumb.

16.   And, behold, *another* **one** like *unto* the simili-
tude of the sons of men, touched my lips. Then I
opened my mouth, and spake and said unto him
that stood before me, O my Lord, by *reason of* the
vision my sorrows are turned upon me, and I have
retained no strength.

17.   For how can the *humble* servant of this my
lord *even* talk with this my lord? For as for me,
straightway there remained no strength in me,
neither is there breath left in me *even now.*

18.   Then there came again and touched me *another* **one** like *unto* the appearance of a man, and he
strengthened me,

19.   And said, O man greatly beloved, fear not. Peace *be* unto thee, be strong *I say*, yea, be strong. And when he had spoken unto me, I was strengthened, and said, Let my lord speak; for thou has strengthened me, *and I am now able to receive thy words.*

20.   Then said he, *Thou* knowest thou wherefore I *am* come unto thee. And now will I return to fight with the *unholy* prince of *the kingdom of* Persia *once again.* And when I am gone forth, lo, *in due time,* the *unholy, overseeing* prince of *the kingdom of* Grecia shall come *in his stead.*

21.   But I will shew *unto* thee, that which is noted in the scripture of truth. And *there is currently* none that holdeth *as closely* with me in these things, but Michael your prince.

CHAPTER 11

1.   Also, I *Gabriel,* in the first year of Darius the Mede, *even* I, stood *up* to confirm and to strengthen him.

2.   And now will I shew *unto* thee the truth. Behold, there shall stand up yet three kings *within the Empire of* Persia, *namely Cyrus, and Cambyses, and Darius I.* And the fourth king, *who is Xerxes,* shall be far richer than *they* all. And by his strength, *and*

through his riches, he shall stir up all *of them to fight,* against the realm of Grecia.

3.   And a mighty *Grecian* king *named Alexander the Great,* shall stand up. *It is he* that shall rule with great dominion, and do according to *all of* his will.

4.   And when he shall stand up, his kingdom shall be *eventually* broken *because of his death at a young age,* and shall be divided toward the four winds of heaven, *which represent his four top generals.* And not to his *own family* posterity, nor according to his *own* dominion which he ruled, *because he will have had no son.* For his kingdom shall be plucked up, even for others beside those.

5.   And *one of his generals, who shall become* the king of the south, *which shall be called Ptolemy I,* shall be strong, and *one* of his princes, *which is named Seleucus I, who is also called Nicator the Conqueror, shall rise.* And he shall be strong above *and beyond* him, and *shall* have dominion. *And* his dominion *shall be* a great dominion.

6.   And in the end of *the* years they shall join themselves together. For the king's daughter of the south, *named Bernice,* shall come to the king of the north, *named Antiochus Theos, in order* to make an agreement *through marriage.* But she shall not retain the power of the arm *of the Syrian throne;* neither shall he stand, nor his arm. But she shall be given

up *and left, and then murdered, in Antioch*, and they that brought her, and he that *even* begat her, and he that strengthened her *shall be killed as well,* in *these* times.

7.   But out of a branch of her roots shall *one* stand up in his estate, *who shall be named Ptolemy III, who was her brother,* which shall come *forth* with an army, and shall enter into the fortress of the king of the north, and shall deal against them *with strength,* and shall prevail.

8.   And shall also carry captives into Egypt; *with those of* their gods, *and* with their princes, *and* with their precious vessels of silver and gold. And he, *namely Ptolemy III,* shall continue *more* years than the king of the north.

9.   So the king of the south shall come *again* into *his own* kingdom, and shall return into his own land *of Egypt.*

10.   But his sons, *namely Seleucus III and Antiochus III* shall be stirred up *to fight,* and shall assemble a multitude of great forces. And *one of them* shall certainly come *forth, namely Antiochus III,* and *shall* over flow, and pass through *the land in the north.* Then shall he return, and be stirred up, *even un*to his *own* fortress *which is in the boarders of Egypt.*

11.   And *in due time,* the king of the south, *which shall be Ptolemy Philopater* shall be moved with choler,

and shall come forth and fight with him, *even* with the king of the north, *which shall be Antiochus the Great of Syria.* And he shall set forth a great multitude; but the multitude *alas,* shall be given into his hand.

12.   *And* when he hath taken away the multitude, his heart shall be lifted up *with pride.* And he shall cast down *many* ten*s of* thousands. But he shall not be strengthened *by doing it.*

13.   For the king of the north, *namely Antiochus the Great of Syria,* shall return, and shall set forth a multitude *even* greater than the former, and shall certainly come after *them for a* certain *number of* years with a great army and with much riches.

14.   And in those times there shall many stand up against the king of the south, *namely Antiochus the Great of Syria, and Philip of Macedonia.* Also the robbers of thy people, *namely the Hebrews who rejected their own religion,* shall exalt themselves to establish the vision; but they shall fall.

15.   So the king of the north, *namely Antiochus the Great of Syria,* shall come and cast up a mount, and *shall* take the most *securely* fenced *of the* cities *within Israel.* And the arms of the south shall not *be able to* withstand, neither *shall* his, *that is, God's,* chosen people *be able to stand,* neither *shall there be any* strength to withstand.

16. But he that cometh against him, *namely Antiochus the Great of Syria coming against Ptolemy Philopater of Egypt,* shall do according to his own will, and none shall *be able to* stand before him. And he shall stand in the glorious land *of Israel,* which by his hand shall be consumed.

17. He shall also set his face to enter with the strength of his whole kingdom *into the land of Egypt,* and *the* upright ones *will be* with him; thus shall he do *it.* And he shall give *unto* him, *that is to Ptolemy Philopater of Egypt,* the daughter of women, *namely his own daughter, Cleopatra,* corrupting her *against Ptolemy.* But she shall not stand *with her father* **on his side,** neither *shall she* be for him.

18. After this shall he turn his face unto the isles *of the Mediterranean Sea,* and shall take many *by force.* But a prince *of the Roman consul,* for his own behalf, shall cause the reproach *that is* offered by him, *that is, by Antiochus the Great of Syria,* to cease. Without his own reproach, he shall cause *the reproach that is offered by Antiochus,* to turn upon him*self.*

19. Then he, *namely Antiochus the Great of Syria,* shall turn his face toward the *security of the* fort of his own land. But he shall stumble and fall, and not be found, *because of his death in an ensuing war with Luristan.*

20.   Then shall stand up in his estate a raiser of taxes *in* the glory of the kingdom, *namely Seleucus IV*. But within *a* few days he shall be destroyed, neither in anger, nor in battle, *but rather he shall be poisoned.*
21.   And in his estate shall stand up a vile person, *namely Antiochus Epiphanes*, to whom they shall not *officially* give the honour of the kingdom. But he shall come in peaceably *instead*, and obtain the kingdom by flatteries.
22.   And with the arms of a flood *of supporters* shall they be overflown from before him, and shall be broken. Yea, *shall* also the prince of the *holy* covenant *be broken and killed, namely Onias the High Priest.*
23.   And after the league *made* with him he shall work deceitfully *against Jason, who replaced Onias as the High Priest.* For he shall come up, and shall become strong with a small *amount of* people.
24.   He shall enter peaceably even upon the fattest places of the province. And he shall do *that* which his fathers have not done, nor his father's fathers *before him.* He shall scatter among them the prey, and *the* spoils, and *the* riches. *Yea*, and he shall forecast his devices against the strong holds, even for a time.
25.   And he, *namely Antiochus Epiphanes* shall stir up his power and his courage against the king of the

south, *namely Ptolemy Philometor,* with a great army. And the king of the south shall be stirred up to battle with a very great and mighty army; but he shall not stand. For they shall forecast devices *of corruption* against him.

26.   Yea, they that feed *him* of the portion of his *own* meat shall destroy him *in the end*, and his army shall overflow; and many shall fall down slain.

27.   And both *of* these kings' hearts *shall be* to do mischief, and they *both* shall speak lies at one table; but it shall not prosper *in the end*. For yet the end *shall be* at the time appointed.

28.   Then shall he, *namely Antiochus Epiphanes* return into his *own* land with great riches. And his heart *shall be* against the *Hebrew people of the* holy covenant *of God*. And he shall do *exploits*, and *then* return *un*to his own land.

29.   At the time appointed he shall return *once again*, and come toward the south. But it shall not be as *victorious as the triumph over Pelusium, which is* the former, or as *his subjugation of all of Egypt, except Alexandria, which was* the latter.

30.   For the ships of Chittim shall come against him *through Roman warnings*. Therefore he shall be grieved *because of having to turn back*, and return, and have indignation against the *Hebrew people of the* holy covenant *of God*. So shall he do. He shall even

return, and have intelligence with them *of the He-brew lineage,* that forsake the holy covenant *of God.*
31.   And arms shall stand on his part, and they shall pollute the sanctuary of strength, and shall take away the *regular* daily **sacrifice** *within the Hebrew holy temple,* and they shall place the abomination *of a slaughtered swine upon the altar,* that maketh *it* desolate.
32.   And such as do wickedly against the *holy* covenant *of God,* shall he corrupt by flatteries. But the people that do know their God shall be strong, and *shall* do **exploits** *under the leadership of the Maccabees.*
33.   And they that *have* understand*ing* among the people shall instruct many. Yet they shall *ultimately* fall by the sword, and by *the* flame, *and* by captivity, and by *the* spoil, *after* many days.
34.   Now when they shall fall, they shall be holpen *up* with *only* a little help. But many shall cleave *un*to them with flatteries.
35.   And **some** of them of understanding shall fall, to try them, and to purge *them,* and to make *them* white, **even** *as un*to the time of the end. Because *it is* for a time appointed *that this is decreed.*
36.   And the king *who is known of as the Antichrist,* shall do according to his *own* will. And he shall exalt himself, and magnify himself above every *other* god, and shall speak marvelous things against the God of gods, and shall prosper till the indignation

be *fully* accomplished. For that *is what is prophesied;* that is *what is* determined *as to what* shall be done.

37.　Neither shall he regard the God of his fathers, nor *demonstrate* the desire *that men have* of women, nor regard any god *other than himself.* For he shall magnify himself above all.

38.　But in his estate shall he *instead,* honour the God of *the natural* forces. And a god whom his fathers knew not shall he honour with gold, and *with* silver, and with precious stones, and *with* pleasant things.

39.　Thus shall he do *abominations* in the most *holy and sacred of* strong holds with a strange god, whom he shall acknowledge *and* increase with glory. And he shall cause them, *that is, strange gods,* to rule over many and shall *share the spoils, and* divide the land for gain, *similar to Antiochus Epiphanes.*

40.　And at the time of the end shall the king of the south, *which is the king of Egypt,* push at him. And the king of the north, *which is the king of Syria,* shall come against him like a whirlwind, with chariots, and with horsemen, and with many ships. And he shall enter into the countries *of the old Grecian Empire,* and shall overflow and pass over *them.*

41.　He shall enter also into the glorious *promised* land *of Israel,* and many **countries** shall be overthrown. But these *three countries* shall escape out of his hand, *even* Edom and Moab, and the chief of the children of Ammon.

42.   *And* he shall stretch forth his hand *militarily* also upon the countries. And the land of Egypt shall not escape.

43.   But he shall *succeed, and* have power over the treasures of *the* gold and of *the* silver, and over all *of* the precious things of Egypt. And the Libyans and the Ethiopians *shall be right there* at his steps.

44.   But *reports and* tidings out of the east and out of the north shall trouble him. Therefore he shall go forth with great fury to destroy *them*, and utterly to take away many.

45.   And he shall plant the tabernacles of his palace *in Jerusalem*, between the seas in the glorious holy mountain *of Mount Moriah*. Yet he shall come to his *complete and utter* end *at Armageddon*, and none shall help him.

CHAPTER 12

1.   And at that time *of the end*, shall *the Archangel* Michael stand up *for Israel*. *He is* the great *angelic* prince which standeth *up* for the children of thy people. And there shall be a time of trouble *and tribulation*, such as *there* never was since there was a nation *on this earth*, *even un*to that same time. And

at that time, *the 144,000 person Manchild of* thy *Chosen* People shall be delivered *from this earth, and from the clutches of the Antichrist, by being raptured into heaven.*

2. And many of them that *are a*sleep *because of death, and buried* in the dust of the earth, shall awake *at the trumpet of the resurrection.* Some *belonging to the first resurrection will awake un*to everlasting life, and some *belonging to the resurrection of damnation, shall awake un*to shame *and* everlasting contempt.

3. And they that be wise, *and choose to receive redemption through the finished work of Christ Jesus,* shall shine as the brightness of the firmament. And they that turn many *away from sin un*to righteousness, *shall radiate* as the stars *of the sky* for ever and ever.

4. But thou, O Daniel, shut up the words *of this prophesy,* and seal *up* the book, *even un*to the time of the end. Many shall run to and fro *in those last days,* and knowledge shall be increased *tremendously.*

5. Then I Daniel looked, and, behold, there stood *an*other two *angels,* the one on this side of the bank of the river, and the other on that side of the bank of the river.

6. And *the one* said to the *divine* man clothed in linen, which *was* upon the waters of the river, How long *shall it be to* the end of these wonders?

7.   And I heard the *divine* man clothed in linen, which *was* upon the waters of the river, when he held up his right hand, and *then* his left hand unto heaven, and sware by him that *sitteth upon the throne, and* liveth for ever *and ever,* that *it shall be* for a time*, and* times, and an half-*time, which is three and one-half years.* And when he shall have accomplished *his purpose* to scatter the power of the holy people *of God*, all these *things* shall be finished.

8.   And I heard *these last days declarations*, but I understood not. Then said I, O my Lord, what *shall be* the end of these *things?*

9.   And he said *unto me*, Go thy way Daniel: for the words *of this prophecy* are closed up and sealed *un*til the time of the end.

10.   Many *people* shall be purified, and made white *through the reality of the new-birth*, and *severely* tried; but the wicked shall *always* do wickedly. And none of the wicked shall *be able to* understand *what is taking place.*

11.   And from the time *that* the daily *sacrifice and the oblations* shall be taken away, and the abomination that maketh desolate set up*, and then finally removed*, **there shall be** a thousand two hundred and ninety days *total.*

12.   Blessed *is* he that waiteth *patiently*, and cometh to the *one*-thousand three hundred*eth* and

five and thirty days *later . . . or five and forty days after the end of the Tribulation Period.*

13.   But go thou thy way *un*til the end *be.* For thou shalt rest *with thy fathers*, and *then* stand in thy lot *with thy people, after thy resurrection,* at the end of the days.

Epilogue

Daniel is a book that was sealed-up by the direction of the Lord of Hosts for centuries. Because of the fact that, within the 21st Century, we are living within the Biblical last days, and we are expecting the return of the Lord Jesus Christ for a "removal from wrath" event at any time, the understanding of the Book of Daniel has been unlocked.

Through the enhancement, we are able to clearly understand early portions of the book, and then readily see the fulfillment of the latter portion of the book taking place right before our very eyes.

We pray that this has been an enjoyable read, and that interest has been generated to look further into the prophetical works contained within the word of God. The compiler of this work has numerous other books, that deal with various issues, from eternity past unto eternity future. We would love to share them with you.

May the grace of the living God cover you like a blanket, and his mercy be demonstrated as these days dwindle down to a precious few.

Maranatha!

Meet the Author

By-The-Book Ministries, Inc. began in 2001 as a teaching outreach. Rob E. Daley has been gifted by God to be able to explain biblical truths in an easy to understand manner.

Many have been blessed by his teaching style.

Rob was saved and filled with the Holy Spirit in 1978 and has been instructed by the greatest teacher of all—the Spirit of Truth Himself. Rob is an ordained minister with the Assemblies of God International Fellowship and has pastored in various churches over the past 34 years.

It is the desire of this ministry to see the body of Christ solidly taught, and grow up into the things of the Lord. Rob is available for seminars, retreats, conventions, etc.

Rob can be reached at:

thedaleys@bythebookministries.org

http://robdaleyauthor.com